ZOO BABIES
Georgie the Giraffe

Story by **Georgeanne Irvine**
Photographs by **Ron Garrison**

of the **Zoological Society of San Diego**

Ideals Publishing Corp.
Milwaukee, Wisconsin

Copyright © MCMLXXXIII
by the Zoological Society of San Diego
All rights reserved. Printed and bound in U.S.A.
Published simultaneously in Canada.

ISBN 0-8249-8053-0

Adult giraffes are the tallest animals in the world. Some of them are over eighteen feet tall! I'm Georgie, a giraffe at the Zoo. Even though I'm only a baby, I'm already six feet tall.

I live with my mom, Jigsaw, my dad, Blackjack, and a herd of other giraffes in the big, open African enclosure at the Zoo. We have a lot of room to roam freely which makes living here almost like living in our native Africa.

We aren't the only animals living in the African enclosure. There are zebras, gnus, ostriches, Cape buffaloes, and many kinds of antelopes. I like living with the other animals now, but it took me a while to get used to them.

Just before I was born, the zoo keepers put Mom in a wooden pen called a boma. When I was born, Mom and I stayed in the boma alone.

The keepers wanted me to live in the boma for about a month until they felt I was strong enough to go out into the big African enclosure.

Mom let me run around, play, explore, and do just about anything I wanted to do in the boma. The other giraffes would come over to visit me because they were curious. They couldn't come into the boma, but they peered in over the wall.

The day came for Mom and me to be released into the big African enclosure. Because I wasn't tall enough to see over the boma walls, I had no idea what it would be like outside. I expected to be with only Mom and the other giraffes.

Was I in for a surprise when I stepped outside the boma! I saw not only giraffes, but all kinds of animals I had never seen before. I was frightened and shy.

Mom said it was all right to be shy because giraffes are naturally shy and quiet. But she said I shouldn't be afraid because the other animals wouldn't hurt me. In the wild, giraffes live peacefully with these other animals, too. Even though I believed her, I stayed very close to her when we began exploring.

First we went over to a thorny acacia tree, and Mom started chewing some leaves. One of the reasons we giraffes are tall is so that we can reach high into treetops. We have an extra-long tongue—about eighteen inches long—to get those almost-out-of-reach leaves. While Mom nibbled on leaves, I kept looking for those other animals.

Next we passed one of my aunts who was bent over with her front legs spread far apart so she could drink water from a pond. Giraffes' legs and necks are so long, the only way we can drink is by standing in this funny-looking position.

I continued to follow Mom. She led me over to a group of my giraffe relatives. All of them stood around me and asked how I liked being out of the boma. I said I thought it was wonderful except that I was frightened to be with all of those other animals.

"This won't do," they said. A couple of them galloped over to a herd of zebras and ostriches. Some of my other relatives joined a group of gnus and antelopes. Nothing happened to any of them! My giraffe relatives and the other animals just stood peacefully together as if they had always been friends.

"OK, Mom," I said. "I feel a lot braver now. If my giraffe relatives can get along with the other animals, then so can I!" With that, I galloped off to make friends with some gnus!